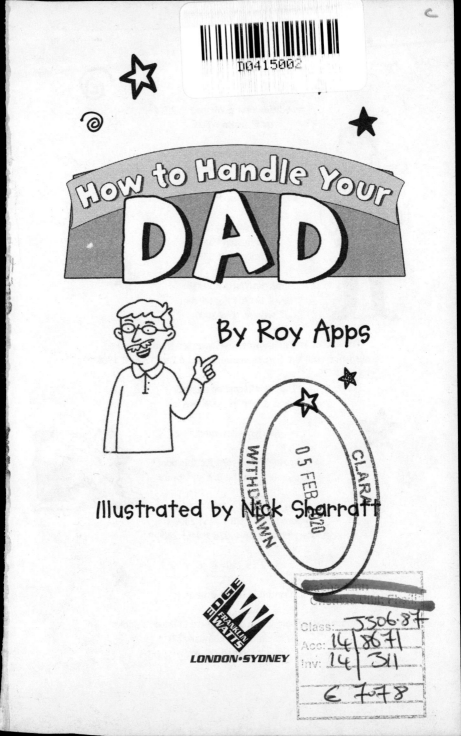

How to Handle Your DAD

By Roy Apps

Illustrated by Nick Sharratt

EDGE

FRANKLIN WATTS

LONDON · SYDNEY

This edition first published in 2014
by Franklin Watts

Text © Roy Apps 2014
Illustration* © Nick Sharratt 2014
Cover design by Cathryn Gilbert
Layouts by Blue Paw Design

Franklin Watts
338 Euston Road
London NW1 3BH

Franklin Watts Australia
Level 17/207 Kent Street
Sydney, NSW 2000

*The Ford Escort on page 27
was drawn by Jo Moore

A CIP catalogue record for this book
is available from the British Library.

(pb) ISBN: 978 1 4451 2396 7
(ebook) ISBN: 978 1 4451 2400 1
(Library ebook) ISBN: 978 1 4451 2404 9

1 3 5 7 9 10 8 6 4 2

Printed in Great Britain

Franklin Watts is a division of Hachette Children's Books,
an Hachette UK company.
www.hachette.co.uk

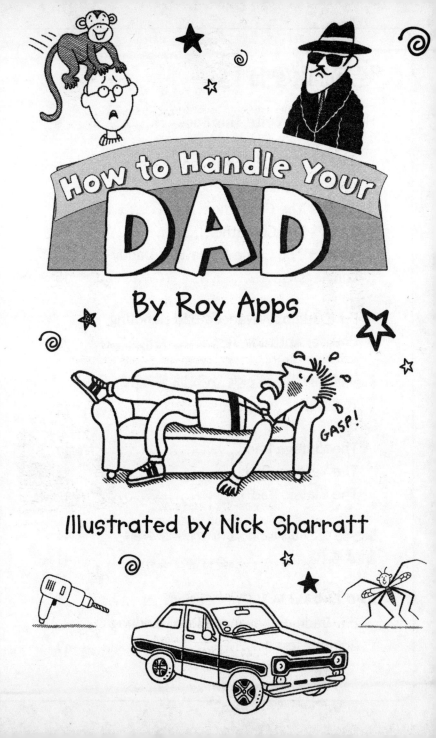

How to Handle Your DAD

By Roy Apps

GASP!

Illustrated by Nick Sharratt

Contents

How I Got To Write This Book

It was a dark and stormy night — which is often how a good book starts...

I was working hard at my desk, when I was suddenly woken up by a strange buzzing in my left ear. It was my phone. I could tell from the number that it was my publisher, Adriano.*

"Hello?" I said.

* The person who actually paid me money to write these words – yes, you can get paid for writing words. Crazy, eh?

"Mr Quizmister. You've got to do something for me! I'm desperate!"

"Oh, hi Des," I replied cheerily.

"No...no! My name isn't Des Perate!"

"Isn't it?"

It was outrageous! Adriano turned into Des, who had turned out to be another telephoney!

"What is your name then?" I asked.

"It's Adriano La Ferminnit. Your publisher. Listen. You must write a book for me about how to handle your dad."

"Must I?"

"Yes! Today!"

"But why should I write a book for you about how to handle my dad when you don't even know him?"

The phone went

Purrrrrr...

Either Adriano La Ferminnit had been cut off, or he'd put his cat on the line to speak to me.

Then I remembered! I had agreed to write a book for Adriano La Ferminnit by 1st January. Then I remembered another something else. It was New Year's Eve tomorrow. I only had a day to write it!

OK, I was panicking, and there was a very good reason my publisher was desperate.

His father had threatened to stop his pocket money for a month unless he did something about tidying up his bedroom. That's why he needed me to write a book on how to handle your dad.

"No problem, Adriano. It's almost finished," I said and ended the call. (I was only on page 9 but I didn't want to panic him, too. Then as well as being desperate, he would be desperately panicked.)

OK, I knew I was going to need help on this book. So I called in some specialist advice:

"In some specialist advice! Here, boy! Come on!"

"Hello?" said the voice on the end of the phone. "E. I. Daddio, Dad Handling Expert speaking." I explained everything to E. I. Daddio, and being the nice chap that he is, he agreed to help (provided I paid him loads of money).

Are Dads Human? Some Really Awful Truths — and Some Really Awful Jokes

You may find this difficult to believe, but there are actually some types of dad that are easy to handle. However, they're rather like a piece of half-cooked steak; that is they're very rare indeed. If you think you've got one of these types of dad, just copy out his "type" from the following pages onto scrap paper. Then stick them where you can easily see them; like the end of your nose.

That way if someone asks you what type of dad you've got, you won't be stuck for an answer, you'll be stuck *to* an answer.

Then you can use the rest of your scrap paper to do some origami.

Da-dum!

Or alternatively to do some 'orridggami. Now where was I? Oh yes, in the middle of page 11. But I'm not now, I'm at the bottom of page 11. The four types of dad that are easy to handle are:

Humph!

Type 1: The Christmas-type Father (a.k.a. Father Christmas)

Four fascinating facts about this dad-type:

1. JOB: They go on lots of business trips to Lapland.

2. FAVE GEAR: Really crazy fur-lined red coats and hats all year round.

3. WHEELS: None. They use a sleigh.

Pull the other one. It's got bells on.

4. FAVE FOOD: Anything, so long as it's not mince pies.

Typical Father Christmas conversation:
YOU: What's that drifting out of the clouds onto our roof, Dad?
FATHER CHRISTMAS: Only rain dear! Ho! Ho! Ho!

Type 2: The Godfather

Four fascinating facts about this dad-type:

1. JOB: They work as violinists, or fiddlers at any rate.
2. FAVE GEAR: Black fur coats and shades. Crazy!
3. WHEELS: Black Mercedes.
4. FAVE FOOD: Steak out.

Typical Godfather conversation:
YOU: Can I come for a ride in the car, Dad?
GODFATHER: Sure. Get in the boot.

Type 3: The Codfather

Four fascinating facts about this dad-type:

1. JOB: Something of-fish-all.

2. FAVE GEAR: Oilskins and waders.

3. WHEELS: Turbot-powered Jeep.

4. FAVE FOOD: A little fishy on a little dishy.

Typical Codfather conversation:

CODFATHER: What do you think of that, eh?

YOU: It's a bit small for bait isn't it, Dad?

CODFATHER: Bait! That's the fish I've just caught!

Type 4: The Crane Fly (a.k.a. Daddy-Longlegs)

Four fascinating facts about this dad-type:

1. JOB: Flying around your head when you're trying to have a shower.
2. FAVE GEAR: T-shirts: preferably down the back of yours.
3. WHEELS: Six legs.
4. FAVE FOOD: Algae and double portion of French flies.

Typical Daddy-Longlegs conversation:
YOU: Aaaaarghhhh!

If your dad's a crane fly, it's incredibly easy to handle him. All you have to do is threaten to fetch the fly swat.

In the incredibly unlikely event that one of

these four dad-types matches the dad you've got, then you can stop reading now. Go on, off you pop. Polish a sleigh or something.

If on the other hand your dad isn't one of these, I'm afraid you need to keep reading.

If you've got a pretty ordinary type of dad, there's no need to worry. Fortunately, help is not very far away. In fact, it's about twenty centimetres away. In front of your eyes. In the pages of this awesome book.

The first thing to establish is what your dad is, now you know that he's not a Santa Claus, a Mafia boss, a fisherman or a crane fly. Now you probably think he's a member of the human race, but nothing could be farther — or indeed *father* — from the truth! The only race your dad's ever likely to be part of is the egg-and-spoon race on school sports day. Have a go at the following quiz:

You questionnaire! I hate you!

I'm going to tell on you! I am! So there!

I didn't mean that sort of having a go, I meant having a go at answering the questions:

Quiz

Record your answers on a scrap piece of paper.

1. You're in the front room with your dad. He's watching a really old film on the telly. You're playing with Freddy, your pet frog. In a corner of the room is a pile of wood — the remains of the bookshelves your dad put up five minutes ago, which have fallen down.

Which of the objects would you describe as creaky?

  A: The old film on the telly
  B: Your dad's bookshelves
  C: Freddy the Frog
  D: Your dad's knees

2. What does your dad
do after going out for
a five-minute jog?

  A: Collapse on the floor?
  B: Collapse on the sofa?
  C: Collapse onto his new bookshelves?

GASP!

3. What does your dad say when your mum asks him if he's going to help her with the weekly shopping?

A: "Aargh! My back! It's killing me!"

B: "Oooh! My leg! It's my hamstring, I think!"

C: "I was just going to try and put those bookshelves up...er...again."

4. Does your dad:

A: Live in a swamp?

B: Have slimy green scales all down his back?

C: Have teeth the size of gravestones?

Answers:

1:

A: Right Answer! That old film is creaky.

B: Right Answer! Those bookshelves are creaky (which is why they fell down).

C: Wrong Answer! Freddy the Frog is really croaky, not really creaky.

D: Wrong answer! Your dad's knees aren't just creaky. They're ~~extremely~~ creaky.

2: If you answered a), b) or c) then, again, your dad isn't a human. He's hardly Iron Man either, is he?

3: If you answered a), b) or c) to question 3 then, once again, your dad isn't a human being. Though he may be a hu-moan being.

And there you have it. Dads tend to be creaky, unable to go very far and not in a fit state to take your mum shopping. I warned you the truth about dads was really awful and

the awful truth of the matter is, of course,
that dads are OLD CROCKS! Unless
you answered a), b) or c) to question 4,
in which case your dad is not an old crock,
but an OLD CROC.

old crock   old croc

In which case, you'd better not let him
catch you reading this book, because he's
likely to bite your head off. There. I warned
you that the jokes were really awful too,
didn't I?

So if you're going to have any chance at all
of learning how to handle your dad, you've
got to think of him not so much as a dear old
pa, but more like a dear old car.

Now if you have trouble handling an old crock car, the solution is easy-peasy. You take it along to the famous Scottish motor engineer A. McHannick.

To be able to help people sort out problems with their old crock dads though, is much more difficult. It requires a person of great skill, intelligence, fortitude, wit, charm and modesty. But that's enough about my fantastic qualities as a human being. Let me tell you about my expert friend, E. I. Daddio. He tours around with his roadshow *Embarrassing Dads*, helping people with all sorts of problems they may have with their old crocks. In other words, he's a Mobile Old Crock Doc.

If you want to know everything there is to know about how to handle your dad, all you need to do is to follow *E.I. Daddio's Advanced Dad Handling Course*. It comes in one easy stage — and one hard stage.

Of course, you do have to be particularly brilliant, intelligent and brainy to take the course. So, just to make sure you're up to it, there is an advanced aptitude test to complete before you begin. The test starts as soon as you turn the page. Good luck!

E.I. Daddios's Advanced Dad Handling Course

APTITUDE TEST

★ Please answer all questions on a separate sheet of scrap paper.

★ Time allowed: A couple of minutes — or if you need longer, a hundred and twenty-one seconds.

1. Write your name.

2. Antidisestablishmentarianism is a very long word. How do you spell it?

Now turn over for the right answers.
(It's better if you turn the book over. Trying to stand on your head can be tricky.)

OK, the answers to the aptitude test are:

1. Your name (not your name, but the words *your name*. Clever, huh?) Take one point if you got this right.

2. It. (This was actually quite a silly answer.) Take one point if you got this right.

WHAT YOUR SCORE MEANS

2 points: Good. Excellent. You are certainly advanced enough to advance to page 26.

1 point: Hmmm, not bad. Go straight to the next page.

0 points: Shucks, that's terrible. You'll have to go back one page, miss a turn and then try again...

E.I. Daddio's Not Very Secret Diary

0830 hours

I woke to the sound of strange ringing above my head. I looked up and saw it was my mobile.

"Hello," said a voice on the end of the mobile when I answered it. "It's Yousuf Inthesea here. I wonder if you could come round and tell me how much my dad is worth?"

Yousuf Inthesea went on to explain that his dad was a VINTAGE old crock. So I picked up a copy of E.I. Daddio's Vintage Crock Fact File, leapt into my van — and made my way to Yousuf's place.

How To Handle Your Dad: Stage 1

E.I. Daddio's Old Crock Fact File:

The Vintage Dad

**Old Crock:
A popular vintage car**

**Old Crock:
A vintage Pop**

Vintage crocks were built between 1960 and 1970, when people used to make do with what they had. Most crocks were fitted with second-hand or used parts. That's why Yousuf's gran says things to his mum about his dad like:

GRAN: I always said he had his Uncle Wazim's ears.

Vintage crocks are also know as (a.k.a.) old bangers. They are known as old bangers for two reasons. The first reason is because their skin resembles that of an ancient sausage, i.e. it's all wrinkly.

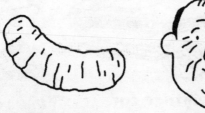

old sausage   **old dad**

The second reason vintage dads are known as old bangers is that they are built from fireworks and can explode at any time. This is what happened when I was in the kitchen with Yousuf. Suddenly his dad came in. Quickly, I realised it was time to retire to a safe distance behind the fridge to watch the display...

DAD: Oh no, I'll be late for work! What's the time, Yousuf?

YOUSUF: It's a device for measuring the length of the day, Dad.

DAD: Grrr! (NOTE HOW HIS EYES START ROLLING LIKE CATHERINE WHEELS.)

DAD: Yee-owww! Who left that drawing pin on the floor? (NOTE HOW HE STARTS LEAPING AROUND LIKE A JUMPING JACK.)

DAD: Put the toaster on!

YOUSUF: I can't, Dad. It won't go over my ears.

DAD: Bahhhh! Yousuf you...! (NOTE HOW HE STARTS HISSING AND SPITTING LIKE A ROMAN CANDLE.)

29

DAD: I meant switch it on!

YOUSUF: No, Dad.

DAD: Then I will!

(NOTE HOW HE SHOOTS ACROSS THE KITCHEN FLOOR LIKE A ROCKET.)

YOUSUF: No, Dad!

DAD: What's wrong with the thing?

YOUSUF: There's a loose—

(NOTE HOW HE THUMPS THE TOASTER. NO, ON SECOND THOUGHTS, TAKE COVER!!!)

BANG!

YOUSUF: —connection.

Oh dear, that blew it — the fuse that is. "I'm still in the dark about how much my dad is worth," said Yousuf.

"We're all still in the dark," I replied. Which was true, because Yousuf's dad was still trying to find his way to the electricity fuse box.

Once the lights were back on, I was able to give Yousuf a copy of my valuation report.

E.I. Daddio's Valuation Report On How Much Vintage Dads Are Worth:

For fifty-one weeks of the year, absolutely zilch. But during the week of 5 November you can make stacks of cash by hiring them out as One-Man Firework Displays.

0900 hours

A regular customer of mine, Annie Oldiron, called. "Can you come round and give my dad an annual checkup?"

"Of course," I replied, "which of his annuals would you like me to check up: *The Beano Annual 1984* or *The One Direction Annual 2013*." Then Annie explained that she wanted to make sure that her dad, who was a VETERAN old crock, wasn't falling to bits.

It was time to hit the road again...

I gave Annie Oldiron a few notes about her veteran dad:

Then after inspecting him, I gave her some more notes about her veteran dad.

E.I. Daddio'S Old Crock Fact File:

The Veteran Dad

A typical veteran dad, a Sko-Da

A posh version of the Sko-Da, a Sko-La-di-Da

Veteran crocks were built between 1970 and 1975. Just as some veteran cars were built so you could feel the sun on your head, so were veteran dads.

Nothing on top   **Nothing on top**

Veteran crock cars have terrible old chokes that make them groan.

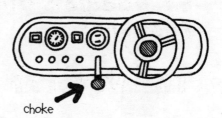

choke

Veteran crock dads have terrible old jokes which make you groan.

How do you make a Swiss Roll?

Push him down a mountain!

Another quaint feature of veteran crocks is their hand signals.

Just tidy that up!

* As you can see, Annie Oldiron's dad does have some hair on top, though. But I've instructed her to check it every day. After all, there's a great deal of truth in the old saying, "Hair today, gone tomorrow".

Off you go, you'll be late for school!

Upstairs to your bedroom!

He's your gerbil, get down there and find him!

There was no doubt about it. Annie Oldiron's veteran dad certainly had a point. In fact, he had about four of them!

1000 hours

It was time to head for the station where I had planned to catch up with Noah Wunsin's classic dad. The reason Noah's dad was at the station was that he was the third type of dad — that is a CLASSIC dad.* However, whereas other classic dads try to keep in condition by weight training, Noah's dad tries to keep in condition by train waiting.

Weight training

Train waiting

Here are a few very useful facts and quite a lot more not very useful facts on this type of old pa.

---

* I hope you're taking all this in, 'cos I shall be asking questions later. On page 40 to be precise.

E.I. Daddio'S Old Crock Fact File:

The Classic Dad

A 4-wheel-drive car — good for driving round bends

A 4-wheel-drive dad — good for driving you round the bend

Classic crocks were built between 1975 and 1985. They are known for their classic lines.

Note the classic lines

Note the lines

All classic crocks are G.T.S. types: that is, Gone To Seed. Although, like Noah's dad they can sometimes look a bit deflated, this isn't really a problem because they always carry a spare tyre:

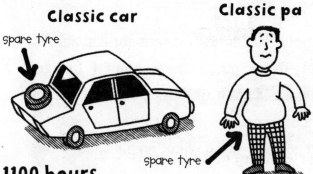

Classic car

spare tyre

Classic pa

spare tyre

1100 hours

It was time for my mid-morning brake...

E.I. DADDIO

MOBILE OLD CROCK DOC.

SCREECH!

Sorry that should've read "time for my mid-morning break". I munched away on some of my favourite dad-type snack: popcorn.

It is also time for you to try your hand at E.I. Daddio's famous Old Crock Spot Check or alternatively, you can try your brain at it:

E.I. Daddio's Old Crock Spot Check:

Is your dad vintage, veteran or classic? It's easy to find out. Just give him E.I. Daddio's famous OLD CROCK DOC spot check by choosing one answer to this question:

What does your dad put on his head in the morning?

A: Tomato ketchup

B: A bowler hat

C: Polish

D: Fertiliser

E: Toothpaste

E.I. Daddio's analysis of what the answers mean:

A: If you've chosen this answer, your dad's an old banger. In other words, a vintage dad.

B: If you've chosen this answer, your dad's not an old banger, but more likely an old banker.

C: If you've chosen this answer, you've got a veteran dad with a chrome dome.

D: If you've chosen this answer, your dad's Gone To Seed: he's a classic.

E: If you've chosen this answer, your dad was still asleep when he went to the bathroom.

How To Handle Your Dad: Stage 2

E.I. Daddio's Advanced Dad Handling Course:

Dads are like an Agony Aunt's blog; they're full of problems. Problems for you, that is. E.I. Daddio's Advanced Dad Handling Course will now take you through the telltale signs, causes and solutions to some of the most common problems, as recorded in E.I. DADDIO's Not Very Secret Diary of an Old Crock Doc.

E.I. Daddio's Not Very Secret Diary

1230 hours

Jim Nasticks called me to say he was having trouble with his dad.

"I'll be round in two shakes of a lamb's tail!" I said.

Unfortunately it took me twenty minutes to find a lamb and then another twenty minutes to catch it so that I could shake its tail.

When I eventually arrived at Jim Nasticks's place, his dad's face spoke volumes:

"Is he about to blow a gasket?" asked Jim.

"You're getting warm," I replied. "Mind you, your dad's getting more than warm."

Yes, Jim's dad was displaying classic symptoms of overheating.

DAD PROBLEM 1: OVERHEATING

LOOK FOR THESE TELLTALE SIGNS:

1. Your dad getting very hot under the collar.
2. Your dad getting very hot under his bonnet (if he wears one).

LISTEN OUT FOR THESE TELLTALE NOISES:

"Grrrr!"   "Borrr!!!"
"Yahhh!!!"

WHAT CAUSES THE PROBLEM:

The slightest thing can cause a dad to overheat. For example, read what happened when I visited Yousuf Inthesea's dad.* Another common cause is too much in the boot.

Who put these bricks in my boot?

"I've not put any bricks in my dad's boots," said Jim. "So what can be causing him to overheat like this?"

We went out to the garden to have another look at Mr Nasticks. As soon as I saw him, the cause of the overheating

*See pages 28–31.

became pretty obvious — or rather not-very-pretty obvious.

"There's no doubt about it, Jim," I said.

"Your dad's labouring in the wrong gear!"

Of course, just as with old cars, overheating results in old pas fuming.

Old car

Old pa

To help Jim Nasticks with his overheating dad, I sent him this guide:

But she turned out to be as much use as a chocolate teapot, so I sent him this guide instead:

E.I. Daddio's Easy Step-By-Step Guide To Stopping Dads From Overheating:

1. **Check seriousness of overheating problems. Is there:**

(i) Steam coming out of his ears?

NO   **YES** ➜ Serious overheating problem, go to 2.

⬇

(ii) Steam coming out of his mouth?

NO   **YES** ➜ Tell him to keep off the Bombay Mix. Go to 2.

⬇

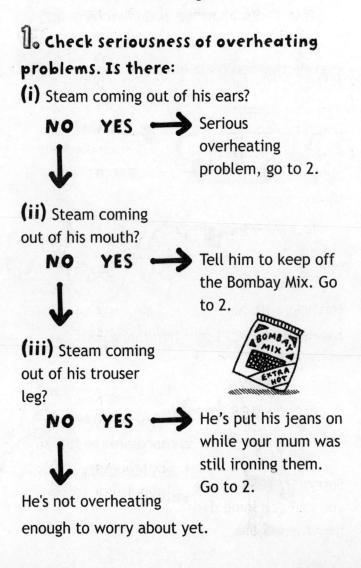

(iii) Steam coming out of his trouser leg?

NO   **YES** ➜ He's put his jeans on while your mum was still ironing them. Go to 2.

⬇

He's not overheating enough to worry about yet.

2. Try these methods to cool him down:

(i) Say: "Father, your tea is cold, would you like another cup?" Has he cooled down?

NO → (down)

YES → Success! Now all you've got to do is find a potter's wheel, a kiln and clay and you'll be able to make your dad another cup.

(ii) Say: "Father dear, I'd love to listen to your wonderful Beatles album." Has he cooled down?

NO → (down)

YES → Success! Now all you've got to do is to find your extra thick ear defenders.

(iii) Turn the hot tap off when he's in the shower. Has he cooled down?

NO → (down)

YES → Success! Now lock yourself in your bedroom for about four weeks.

Sorry! There's nothing you can do. Some dads never get cool.

Useful Tool For Dealing With Overheating Dads:

A HOSE-PIPE: Particularly useful for trying to cool your dad down, if you haven't got a shower. Also, it means you can earn yourself some extra pocket money as a decorator. All you need to do is to shove the hose-pipe in your dad's ear while he's got a full head of steam, so to speak, and use your hose-pipe as a wallpaper stripper.

Before moving on to the next entry from E.I. Daddio's Not Very Secret Diary of an Old Crock Doc, complete the following test on OVERHEATING:

E.I. DADDIO'S ADVANCED DAD HANDLING COURSE: TEST 1

QUESTION: Which of the following things causes a dad to overheat?

A: Wearing a woolly vest in the middle of June.

B: Wearing a woolly vest in the middle of Wilkinson's.

C: Labouring in the wrong gear.

D: Too much in the boot.

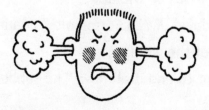

Answers:

A: No points, but 10 pints. Of lemonade, that is, for your dad to help him cool down.

B: This is more likely to cause you to overheat — with embarrassment.

C: 1 point.

D: Another point.

E.I. Daddio's Not Very Secret Diary

1300 hours

The phone rang. My publisher, Adriano La Ferminnit was on the line.

"Get down, Mr La Ferminnit!" I called to him out of the window.

"I want to end it all now!" he sobbed.

"Surely, Mr La Ferminnit, it's not that bad!"
I replied.

"Oh, yes it is," he said. "Particularly that
joke on page 45 about labouring in the wrong
gear."

"That was no joke," I said. "At least, it
wasn't for Jim Nasticks."

"Will you promise that the rest of your book
will be serious — in particular, no more puns?"

"OK," I agreed, "no more puns, just bitta
pread, puttered scones and paps."

Next to call was another
regular customer of mine, Jilly
Concarny. "It's my dad," she said,
"I can't get him to budge at all."

When I got to Jilly Concarny's house, she took me into the lounge to see her dad.
But I couldn't.
See him, that is.

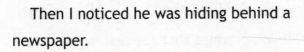

Then I noticed he was hiding behind a newspaper.

"Is it an expensive problem?" asked Jilly.

"Oh dear," I said.

"Is it?" said Jilly. "Well, I haven't got a lot of money."

"Don't worry," I told her. "I'll soon get your dad started."

DAD PROBLEM 2: GETTING STARTED

LOOK OUT FOR THESE TELLTALE SIGNS:
Your dad won't budge. Your appeals for a new bike/horse/game of football/month's holiday in Disneyland/help with your maths homework, etc. seem to leave him completely unmoved!

LISTEN OUT FOR THESE TELLTALE NOISES:

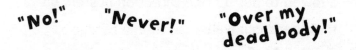

"No!"   "Never!"   "Over my dead body!"

WHAT CAUSES THE PROBLEM:
Like really old cars, old dads have to be started with what's known as a crank handle.

crank

This is hardly surprising, as dads tend to have some cranky ideas. For example:

YOU SAY: Why have you turned the telly off, Dad?
DAD SAYS: Your homework is more  important than catching up with *Hollyoaks*!
YOU THINK: Cranky idea!

YOU SAY: But, Dad! Everyone else is allowed to put up One Direction posters on their bedroom wall.
DAD SAYS: Yes, but not on the outside!
YOU THINK: What's his problem?

YOU SAY (as you come in from school): Hi, Dad.
DAD SAYS: Hello,  sweetheart! Did you have a really exciting day at school?
YOU THINK: His mind's going.

Now, in some ways old dads are more like old clocks than old crocks.

That is, you have to wind them up.

SOLUTION: E.I. Daddio's Most Commonly Used Dad Wind-ups:

WIND-UP 1

YOU: Dad! Gran's on the phone. She wants to come and stay for a month.

DAD (wound up nicely now): Aargh! Tell her we're moving to the Outer Pollywollydoodle Islands!

YOU: But I've got my maths homework to do!

RESULT: Your dad starts doing your maths homework...

AT LEAST UNTIL...
He remembers that your gran is already staying with you.

WIND-UP 2

YOU: Dad! The bloke next door is just about to use a chainsaw on your prize monkey puzzle tree.

DAD (wound up nicely now): Right! Here I come...! (Dashes out the back.)

YOU (once outside): Oh! He seems to have gone. Now you're out here though, you can mend my bike, etc.

RESULT: Your dad mends your bike, etc...

AT LEAST UNTIL...

He remembers that he hasn't got a prize monkey puzzle tree — only a prize monkey, i.e. your big brother.

WIND-UP 3

YOU: Dad! Have you seen that Man United have got a new away strip?

DAD (wound up nicely now): That's the fifteenth this season!

YOU: All my mates have got the strip. (Quickly act as though you've lost the FA Cup.)

RESULT: Your dad gives you some extra pocket money...

AT LEAST UNTIL...

He remembers that you're an Arsenal fan.

Useful Spares To Have If Your Dad Tends To Suffer From Starting Problems:

A SPARE YES–U–CAN: Particularly useful when your dad keeps saying "No-You-Can't". Just unlock his fuel cap (if he wears one) and fill up.

E.I. DADDIO'S ADVANCED DAD HANDLING COURSE: TEST 2

QUESTION 1: A handle for starting an old car and a vintage pa can both be described by the same word. Is the word:

   i) crank, **ii)** knarc or **iii)** banger.

QUESTION 2: Can you unscramble these three items that are helpful in Dad wind-ups?

   A: Your NARG, **B:** The KLOBE next door,
C: The new NAM NITDUE away strip.

E.I. Daddio's Not Very Secret Diary

1430 hours

The phone rang. It was my publisher Adriano La Ferminnit. Again.

"Do you know what the time is?" he asked.

"Two thirty," I replied.

"Does it?" he answered. "You'd best get yourself to the dentist then."

No sooner had I put the phone down than I heard someone hammering on the front door.

I went out and spoke to him. "Kindly put that hammer away," I said.

"All right," said the boy who was standing there, "but only if you come round and take a look at my dad. I'm having such dreadful problems with him."

"Jump into the van," I said.

The boy shook my hand. "Noel Plates," he said.

"That's because I've passed my driving test," I replied somewhat huffily.

"No," said the boy, "that's my name. Noel Plates."

When we got to Noel Plates's house, I could hear his dad, even before we got in the front door. In the kitchen, the situation was like a writer of fairy stories: in other words, grim. Noel's dad was holding a bunch of flowers and singing a really soppy song called "Bridge Over Troubled Water" to Noel's mum.

"The problem with your dad," I whispered to Noel, "is that he's rather like the troubled water he's singing about. He's wet. Yes, your dad is suffering —"

"And he's not the only one," butted in Noel.

"— from wet plugs," I said.

DAD PROBLEM 3: WET PLUGS

LOOK OUT FOR THIS TELLTALE SIGN:
Your dad's eyes start to look all moony.

LISTEN OUT FOR THESE TELLTALE NOISES:

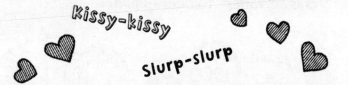

kissy-kissy

slurp-slurp

Your dad starts to make these really wet sounds just when you've got your best friend round. It's so embarrassing!

WHAT CAUSES THE PROBLEM:

Not so much what, as who, because very often the cause of the problem is your mum. If your dad has a tendency to get wet plugs, it's very obvious: you can hear it. One of the most common times your dad will get wet plugs is on a Friday night. He'll come home from work with a bunch of flowers for your mum and you'll hear:

YOUR DAD
(to your mum): Hi, my sweetheart, my pettikins! I'm home.
(KISS. KISS. SLURP. SLURP.) Mmmm…!
YOU THINK: He sounds awful! So wet!

Your mum cooking him his favourite dinner also causes wet plugs.

YOUR DAD (to your mum): Oh, my loveykins! Mmmm… My favourite dinner! Nut and poppy seed salad!

YOU THINK: He sounds awful! So wet!*

E.I. Daddio's Remedies For A Dad With Wet Plugs

QUICK REMEDY:

DRY HIS WET PLUGS:
By turning his
hairdryer on him.

DISADVANTAGE OF
THIS REMEDY: Your
dad probably hasn't got
any hair let alone a hairdryer.

* But not as awful nor as wet as the nut and poppy seed salad.

NOT-SO-FAST REMEDY: JUMP START

YOUR DAD (to your mum): Oh, my loveykins! My favourite! Nut and poppy seed salad.

YOU THINK: He sounds awful! So wet! NOW*!!!* Start jumping up and down.

YOUR DAD: What's wrong with you?

YOU: It's all this bird food you keep giving me. I think I'm turning into an angry bird!

RESULT: Your dad stops calling your mum soppy things like pettikins, etc. and starts calling you stroppy things like nitwit, bird brain, etc.

E.I. DADDIO'S ADVANCED DAD HANDLING COURSE: TEST 3

QUESTION: Which of the following words and noises indicate that your dad has got wet plugs?

A: pettikins!
B: pottikins!
C: slurp
D: burp
E: sweetheart
F: sweat heart

ANSWERS:

A: 1 point.

B: No points. This is what you call your dad after he's tried explaining one of his cranky ideas.

C: 1 point.

D: No points. Your dad's been at that nut and poppy seed salad again.

E: 1 point.

F: No points. This is what your mum probably calls your dad if he's been wearing a woolly vest in June. (See Test 1.)

E.I. Daddio's Not Very Secret Diary

1500 hours

The phone rang again.

"Hello, it's Jilly again," said the voice.

"Well, wear a coat and gloves then," I replied.

"No, it's Jilly Concarny. I rang earlier."

"So you are. Are you still having problems getting your dad started?"

"No, just the opposite. I'm having problems stopping him. He just keeps going on and on."

"Sounds like his battery," I said.

"Please hurry," said Jilly.

"Don't worry," I reassured her, "I'll be with you just as soon as I've finished this...

...sentence."

DAD PROBLEM 4: BATTERY

LOOK OUT FOR THIS TELLTALE SIGN:
Your dad just goes on...and on...and on.

LISTEN OUT FOR THESE TELLTALE SIGNS:

Blah...blah...blah...blah...

WHAT CAUSES THE PROBLEM:
Unlike a car battery which goes flat, the problem with a dad's battery is just the opposite. A dad's battery is long life, in other words, it enables your dad to go on...

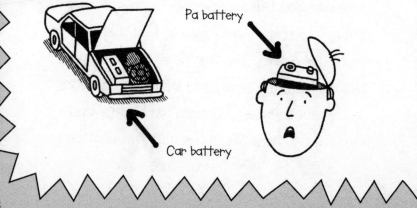

Pa battery

Car battery

...and on...and on... So, an innocent and inoffensive little remark on your part will set him going on and on. For example:

YOU: Dad, can I have the next generation PlayBox? It's out tomorrow with the new *Need For Speed 13* game. Er...please?

DAD: You want another console?

YOU: Yes, please. It only costs a few hundred pounds—

DAD: How much? When I was your age I had to make do with a *Look and Learn Annual* every Christmas, and I had to buy that myself from the money I earned doing thirteen paper rounds before school, and that was a twelve mile walk there and fifteen back — my dad never gave me a lift in the car, and another thing we never had central heating, just a second-hand candle in a broken jam jar that all the family used to huddle round to try and ward off frostbite...blah...drone...blah...

E.I. Daddio's Easy Step-By-Step Guide To Dealing With The Problem Of Classic Dads Who Go On...And On... And On...

1: Take one large balloon.

2: As your dad starts to speak, hold it in front of his mouth.

3: As he talks, the balloon will begin to fill with all his hot air!

4: Now, quickly tie the balloon firmly

Blah blah...

round his middle and under his armpits. (He won't notice, because he'll be too busy telling you about the bad old, good old days.)

5: Once the balloon is filled, tie the end.

6: Now watch your dad float up and away, leaving you in peace to watch the telly, use the hall as a rollerskating alley, clean your bike in the bath, think of another way of asking him about that new console, etc.

Blah blah...

Bye bye!

Useful Spares To Carry If Your Dad Suffers From Battery Problems:

A SPARE SET OF PLUGS: To shove in your ears so you don't have to hear what he's drivelling on about. Pardon? I said:

SHOVE! IN! YOUR! EARS!

Oh never mind, just get on with the next test!

E.I. DADDIO'S ADVANCED DAD HANDLING COURSE: TEST 4

QUESTION: What is a dad with battery problems likely to be full of?

A: a fund of wonderful stories about his childhood

B: hot air

C: polyunsaturates

E.I. Daddio's Not Very Secret Diary

1600 hours

When the mobile rang again, I heard a voice that sounded vaguely familiar.

"Hello. E.I. Daddio Old Crock Doc Extraordinaire. How can I help you?" it said. Then I realised why the voice sounded vaguely familiar — it was mine.

"My name is Willie Woanty," said a voice on the other end of the phone.

"Oh dear, I am sorry," I said.

"It's my dad," he said.

"What's the problem with him?" I asked.

"The problem's not so much with him

73

as with what he's wearing," sighed Willie. Straightaway I knew what the trouble was.

"Your dad's got gearbox problems," I said.

DAD PROBLEM 5: GEARBOX

LOOK OUT FOR THIS TELLTALE SIGN: Your dad coming down the stairs looking like this:

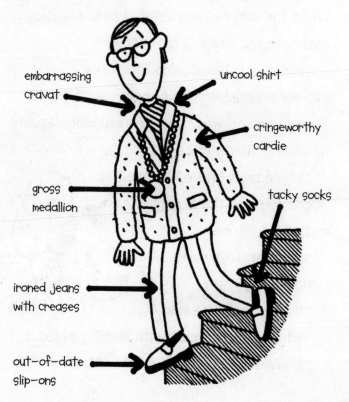

embarrassing cravat

uncool shirt

cringeworthy cardie

gross medallion

tacky socks

ironed jeans with creases

out-of-date slip-ons

LISTEN OUT FOR THIS TELLTALE NOISE:

You are standing in the hall, just about to leave to go to your school parents' evening, when you hear a hideous clunking sound.

WHAT CAUSES THE PROBLEM:

There is obviously something wrong with his gearbox — or as it's sometimes known, his wardrobe. To be more precise, there's something wrong

A car's gearbox

with what's inside his wardrobe. To put it in technical terms,

Your dad's gearbox

car gearboxes have something called synchromesh. Your dad's gearbox is more like synchromess. If your dad is a banger, then this problem can be especially serious, because it means he is likely to have at least one woolly cardie in his gearbox.

Even worse off are people whose dads are codfathers.* These dads always have a kipper tie in their gearbox.

If, on the other hand, your dad comes down the stairs looking like this:

...there is only one explanation.

Your dad is none other than Pop-along Cassidy, the famous cowboy.

Yee-ha!

E.I. Daddio's Tips For Dealing With Your Dad's Gearbox Problems:

!!! Warning !!!

Whatever you do, don't let your dad look in the mirror. You might think that him seeing how ridiculous he looks will bring him to his

*See page 14.

senses. However, it it more likely to bring him to his knees, turn any hair he's got left white and leave him a gibbering wreck as he gazes upon the full horror of what he is wearing.

Aaargh!

HOW TO GET YOUR DAD A NEW GEARBOX:
Getting your dad some gear that's smarter than what he's wearing — without it using up your pocket money — is easy. All you have to do is to find a field with a scarecrow in. Anything the scarecrow's wearing is bound to be smarter than your dad's gear.

Caw

Useful Accessories If Your Dad Needs a New Gearbox:

A CHROME HUBCAP: very handy if you've got a veteran dad with nothing on top: it'll cover up his shiny dome nicely. What's more, it's bound to be an improvement on the cap he wears already.

E.I. DADDIO'S ADVANCED DAD HANDLING COURSE: TEST 5

QUESTION: Match the clothes from these dads' gearboxes to the types of dad that might own them:

a) kipper tie   **b)** cardigan   c) skirt

Dad types:

(i) an old banger

(ii) a dad who has G.T.S. (Gone To Seed)

(iii) a codfather

1 point for each correct pair.

ANSWERS:

a) = (iii) He's probably got a herring-bone jacket as well.

b) = (i) At least it keeps your Gran busy knitting.

c) = (ii) Now you know what the seed he's gone to grows into.

E.I. Daddio's Not Very Secret Diary

I'm Dopey!

1630 hours

I was just settling down to watch Snow White when the phone rang again.

"Hello," I said. "How may I help you?"

"My name's Gail—"

"Not Gail Warning, by any chance?"

"That's right!"

"I rather guessed it might be."

"It's my dad. He's fishing around for something."

"He's not a codfather, is he?"

"No. I mean, he keeps trying to look in my room."

The problem with Gail's father was obvious.

"Ah. I think I know what the problem is, Gail."

"You do?"

"Yes, it's staring you right in your face. Or rather more accurately, it's staring you right in front of your dad's face."

DAD PROBLEM 6: HOOTER

LOOK OUT FOR THIS TELLTALE SIGN:
On an old crock car, you find the hooter on the door. With an old crock dad, you find the hooter peering round the door — the door to your room, that is.

old car's hooter

old pa's hooter

LISTEN OUT FOR THIS TELLTALE NOISE:
You might hear your dad go *Parp! Parp!* but more likely you'll see him go *Peep! Peep!* into your bedroom when he thinks you're not looking.

WHAT CAUSES THE PROBLEM:
It's obvious really: your dad's noticed how good you've been getting at handling him,

so he is desperate to get his hands on
this book!

E.I. Daddio's Solution To The Hooter Problem:

USE A TOE ROPE: Simply tie a length of rope
across your doorway. When your dad next

peeps into your
room, his toe
will stumble
up against
it and he
will trip
over onto his
hooter. This will
stop him peeping, but not parping.

Eek!

DISADVANTAGE OF USING A TOE ROPE:
Unfortunately, as you go racing up the stairs
to your room to read the next bit of *How To
Handle Your Dad*, in your excitement you are

likely to forget that you've set up the toe rope, so you will be tripped up too.

"Eek!"

A Useful Tool To Have If Your Dad Has A Hooter Problem:

MONKEY WRENCH: A monkey is very useful for wrenching your dad away from your bedroom door. They'll try all manner of tricks, e.g. pulling your dad's shoelaces undone, swinging from the chandelier in the hall, jumping off the top of the door onto your dad's head. Of course, it will be a wrench for your dad, but

he'll just have to call a halt to his search for your copy of *How To Handle Your Dad*, while he deals with the monkey.

E.I. DADDIO'S ADVANCED DAD HANDLING COURSE: TEST 6

On a scrap piece of paper, fill in the right words in the gaps:

parp peeps mad dad

Your ..... 's hooter goes ..... when it ..... around your bedroom door and that really makes you .....

One point for parp, one point for peeps, one point for mad and one point for dad.

E.I. Daddio's Not Very Secret Diary

1700 hours

I was just climbing out of my van — when I spotted a figure.

I recognised it immediately. It was 07986100XXX — my phoney number. (You didn't honestly expect me to give out my actual phone number here?)

It was on the side of my van. Then I noticed another familiar figure, running towards me. It was a regular customer of mine: Seeta Down.

"How are you, Seeta?" I asked her.

"I'm...hah...I'm...hah...out...hah...of...
hah...puff," she gasped.

"Here. Have one of mine," I said, digging
deep into a box from my van.

"It's a sugar puff."

No sooner had I given
Seeta a sugar puff, than
another figure came
bounding round the corner.

"Seeta! What do you
think you're doing?" he
yelled.

"It's my dad!" cried Seeta.

"You've got a problem with your dad,
Seeta," I said. "A serious problem known to all
mobile Old Crock Docs as 'running on'!"

DAD PROBLEM 7: RUNNING ON

LOOK OUT FOR THIS TELLTALE SIGN:
Your dad runs after you when you don't want him to.

LISTEN OUT FOR THESE TELLTALE NOISES:
"(YOUR NAME HERE), what do you think you're doing with my **a)** Rolling Stones CD set, **b)** silk dressing gown, **c)** electric drill?"

WHAT CAUSES THE PROBLEM:
Your dad seems to find it totally unreasonable that you are trying to borrow **a)** his Rolling Stones CD set because you've lost your frisbee,

b) his silk dressing gown to take your bike to bits on, to save making the front room carpet dirty, **c)** his electric drill for a game of Robodentist 3.

E.I. Daddio's Solution To Running On Problems:

Remove your dad's fan belt. That way, he'll be too busy trying to hold his trousers up to run on after you.

Useful Tool To Have If You Have A Dad Who's Running On:

WHEEL BRACES: Wheel braces for old crock cars look like this:

Wheel braces for old crock pas look like this.

→

If you can get a pair of wheel braces for your dad for Christmas or his birthday, the benefits will be enormous. Firstly, your dad will be touched (at first, until you ask him for some dosh to buy your mum's Christmas present as you've spent all your pocket money buying his). Secondly, when your dad wears them you'll have no more running on problems with him. All you need to do, when you suspect your dad is about to run on after you, is to make sure the back of his wheel braces are hooked round a door handle. Then, as your dad starts running, the wheel braces will

until they eventually ping him back to the door.

Further details on this technique are revealed in my booklet *How to Door Handle Your Dad*.

E.I. DADDIO'S ADVANCED DAD HANDLING COURSE: TEST 7

QUESTION 1: Match the following things that you are trying to borrow from your dad with what you are trying to borrow them for:

A: electric drill
B: his Rolling Stones CD set
C: his silk dressing gown

i: to replace your lost frisbee

ii: for a game of Robodentist

iii: to take your bike to bits on

QUESTION 2: Match these noises to the
dad problems with which they are associated:

A: Grrrr!   **i:** wet plugs

B: Blah!   **ii:** hooter

C: Peep   **iii:** overheating

D: Slurp!   **iv:** battery

Take one point for each
correct answer, but be careful where
you put it, because they're very sharp.

How I Finished This Book

It was another dark and stormy night, and I was working hard at my desk, when I was suddenly woken up by a strange ringing in my left ear. It was the phone. As you've probably guessed by now, I'm always going to sleep with my phone in my ear.

"Is that you?" asked the voice at the other end.

"No, it's me. Who is that?"

"Your publisher, Adriano La Ferminnit. Don't you recognise my voice?"

"Er...not when it's written down, no," I admitted.

"What does your watch say?" asked my publisher.

tic
tic

"Umm...let me see. Oh yes, Casio," I replied.

"I mean, it's New Year's Eve and it's one minute to midnight. You've got sixty seconds to finish your book on *How To Handle Your Dad*!"

"No, no, that's not right," I said. "I've got fifty-four seconds to finish my book on *How To Handle Your Dad*. But don't worry, I'm almost at the end."

"Grrr!" said my publisher, sounding very much like an overheating vintage dad. "And I'm almost at the end...of my tether."

"Can't you send out for another one?"
I suggested.

"Gah! Look," said Adriano La Ferminnit. He
sounded frantic. "The problems I'm having

with my dad are driving me crazy! There's
smoke coming out from under his bonnet,
I asked him for more pocket money but he
won't budge, he's been singing 'Bridge Over

Troubled Water' to my mum since tea time, he's just going on and on, wearing a really dreadful tie, trying to peer into my room and, oh no...I think he's trying to run after me, just because he knows I'm on the phone to you!"

"I'm afraid I simply must stay here and finish the book, but I'll send one of my apprentices along. They've just been reading the book and are really quite expert Old Crock Docs by now."

"All right, but hurry...!"

Go on! That's right, you! You should be able to work out the problems my publisher is having with his dad. Get round to his place would you? His address is in the front of the book.

Thanks. Now with any luck, by the time you get back I'll have finished typing out the last—

Drat, I've run out of pages...

Teachers make you work hard.
Teachers are always showing off
...and teachers are like machines –
they **never** stop.

Like most teachers, yours is probably an out-of-date robot. And like
most kids, you probably think they'll never run out of batteries...

That's where you're soooo wrong.

How to Handle Your Teacher is here to "help" with all your
teacher-related troubles. Soon you'll have your very own fully
reprogrammed teacher to control!